Edition Schott

T0077175

Paul Hindemith

1895 – 1963

Sonata

für Posaune und Klavier
for Trombone and Piano

Nach dem Text der Ausgabe Paul Hindemith. Sämtliche Werke herausgegeben von /
Edited from the text Edition Paul Hindemith. Sämtliche Werke by
Luitgard Schader

ED 3673
ISMN 979-0-001-04395-3

www.schott-music.com

Mainz · London · Berlin · Madrid · New York · Paris · Prague · Tokyo · Toronto
© 1942/2015 SCHOTT MUSIC GmbH & Co. KG, Mainz · Printed in Germany

Vorwort

Hindemiths *Sonata for Trombone and Piano* entstand 1941 im amerikanischen Exil. In den Jahren der Weimarer Republik stand Hindemith im Zentrum des deutschen Musiklebens. Unter der nationalsozialistischen Diktatur wurde er als „entarteter Künstler" diffamiert. Nur wenige Interpreten setzten seine Kompositionen in Deutschland auf ihr Programm, im Oktober 1936 erließ der Staatssekretär Walther Funk sogar ein generelles Aufführungsverbot für die Werke Paul Hindemiths. Als Bratschen-Virtuose erhielt er in Deutschland keine Engagements, von seiner Professur an der Berliner Musikhochschule ließ er sich mehrfach beurlauben, um im Ausland zu arbeiten. Schließlich zogen Paul und Gertrud Hindemith im September 1938 nach Bluche in der Schweiz. Zwei Jahre später nahm Hindemith eine Professur an der renommierten Yale University in New Haven, im Bundesstaat Connecticut, an.

Schon immer war Hindemiths kompositorisches Schaffen am Bedarf orientiert. Als ihm in der Zeit der politischen Angriffe große Aufführungen unmöglich waren, schrieb er überwiegend kammermusikalische Stücke, die in Deutschland im privaten Bereich gespielt wurden und im Ausland für viele Virtuosen interessant waren. Er begann 1935 – nach einer Unterbrechung von elf Jahren – eine Reihe von Sonaten zu komponieren. Das erste Werk war die *Sonate in E für Geige und Klavier*, das letzte die *Sonate für Basstuba und Klavier* (1955). Zu dieser Reihe gehören neben Sonaten für Streicher, Klavier, Orgel und Harfe auch zehn Sonaten für ein Blasinstrument mit Klavier. Nur einige dieser Stücke schrieb Hindemith für einen besonderen Anlass oder für bestimmte Interpreten. Offensichtlich verfolgte er primär den Plan, für möglichst alle Orchesterinstrumente eine Sonate zu schreiben. Damit wollte er einerseits den Instrumentalisten ein zeitgenössisches Werk geben, andererseits reizte ihn die Aufgabe, für jedes Instrument passend zu komponieren. 1939 erklärte Hindemith seinem Verleger: *Du wirst Dich wundern, daß ich das ganze Blaszeug besonate. Ich hatte schon immer vor, eine ganze Serie dieser Stücke zu machen. Erstens gibt es ja nichts Vernünftiges für diese Instrumente, die paar klassischen Sachen ausgenommen, es ist also zwar nicht vom augenblicklichen Geschäftsstandpunkt, jedoch auf weitere Sicht verdienstlich, diese Literatur zu bereichern. Und zweitens habe ich, nachdem ich mich nun schon mal so ausgiebig für die Bläserei interessiere, große Lust an diesen Stücken.* Besonders in der Zurückgezogenheit des Exils genoss Hindemith die Hausmusik mit seiner Ehefrau. Er spielte dabei gerne Blasinstrumente und berichtete seinem Verleger unter anderem vom *ausgiebig frequentierten Horn und Fagott*, Gertrud Hindemith begleitete ihn am Klavier oder Cello.

Die *Sonata for Trombone and Piano* wurde am 6. Oktober 1941 vollendet. Hindemith hatte die Partitur so sauber geschrieben, dass die amerikanische Verlagsvertretung des Schott-Verlags das Werk direkt als Kopie seiner Handschrift veröffentlichen konnte. Ein Exemplar dieser Ausgabe ließ Hindemith seinem deutschen Verleger nach Mainz schicken. Dort erschien noch während des Zweiten Weltkriegs eine deutsche Ausgabe der Sonate unter dem Titel *Sonate für Posaune und Klavier*. So kam die Sonate auf beiden Kontinenten in den Handel, ohne dass eine offizielle Uraufführung stattfand.

Hindemith zitiert in der Sonate ein Lied, das er in zwei Sprachen nennt, nämlich *Swashbuckler's Song* und *Lied des Raufbolds*. Dieses Lied ist jedoch weder in den Vereinigten Staaten noch in Deutschland als Volkslied bekannt. Sicher ist, dass der Komponist den deutschen Titel zuerst notiert hatte und mit einem Lektor aus New York eine sinnvolle Übersetzung suchte. Aus einem seiner Briefe wissen wir, dass das Zitat *ein wenig komisch gemeint* ist.

Die *Sonata for Trombone and Piano* ist 2014 in Band V,3 der Ausgabe Paul Hindemith. Sämtliche Werke erschienen. In der *Einleitung* sind weitere Informationen zur Entstehungsgeschichte und Rezeption der Komposition zusammengestellt.

Luitgard Schader

Preface

Hindemith's Sonata for Trombone and Piano was written in 1941, while he was in exile in the USA. In the years of the Weimar Republic Hindemith was at the centre of German musical life, but under the National Socialist dictatorship he was vilified as a 'degenerate artist'. Very few performers in Germany featured his compositions in their programmes; in 1936 Secretary of State Walther Funk actually banned the performance of works by Paul Hindemith. There were no bookings for him in Germany as a virtuoso viola player and he took several periods of leave from his post as a professor at the Berlin Academy of Music to work abroad. Paul and Gertrud Hindemith eventually moved to Bluche in Switzerland in September 1938. Two years later Hindemith was appointed as a professor at the prestigious university of Yale in New Haven, Connecticut.

Hindemith's output as a composer had always been determined by demand. When political attacks made large-scale performances impossible he focused chiefly on writing chamber pieces that were played in private houses in Germany and attracted interest from many virtuoso players abroad. In 1935 – after an interval of eleven years – he began to compose a series of sonatas. The first work was the Sonata in E for violin and piano and the last the Sonata for bass tuba and piano (1955). Besides sonatas for strings, piano, organ and harp the series also included eleven sonatas for a wind instrument with piano. Hindemith only wrote a few of these pieces for a particular occasion or a specific performer: his primary intention was evidently to write a sonata each for as many different orchestral instruments as possible. On the one hand he wanted to provide instrumentalists with contemporary music, while on the other hand he welcomed the challenge of composing something to suit each instrument. In 1939 Hindemith announced to his publisher: 'You may be surprised at my writing sonatas for all these wind instruments. I had always intended to produce an entire series of such pieces. Firstly, there is nothing of any substance for these instruments apart from a few classical pieces, so although it may not make good business sense at the moment, it will be worthwhile in the long term to extend the repertoire. Secondly, having taken such a thorough interest in wind instruments, I really enjoyed writing these pieces.' In exile from public life Hindemith enjoyed playing music at home with his wife: as he told his publisher, he would often play wind instruments, f.e. horn and bassoon, with Gertrud Hindemith accompanying him on the piano or cello.

The Sonata for Trombone and Piano was completed on 6 October 1941. Hindemith had written the score out so clearly that the American publishing agents for Schott were able to print the work simply as a copy of his manuscript. Hindemith had one copy of this edition sent to his German publisher in Mainz; a German edition of the sonata was published there before the end of the Second World War under the title *Sonate für Posaune und Klavier*. The sonata thus went on sale on two continents without having been performed in public.

In the Sonata Hindemith quotes a song referred to in two languages, namely *Swashbuckler's Song* and *Lied des Raufbolds*. This song is not known as a familiar folksong, however, either in the United States or in Germany. The composer is known to have noted down the German title first and worked with his editor from New York to find a reasonable translation. We know from one of his letters that the quotation was 'meant to be rather comical'.

This Sonata for trombone and piano appeared in volume V,3 of the complete Hindemith edition in 2014. The introduction there includes further information on the background and critical response to this composition.

Luitgard Schader
Translation Julia Rushworth

Sonata for Trombone and Piano

Als Erstausgabe der Sonate erschien eine Kopie von Hindemiths Manuskript.
The first edition of the Sonata was a copy of Hindemith's manuscript.

Sonata

Paul Hindemith
1895–1963

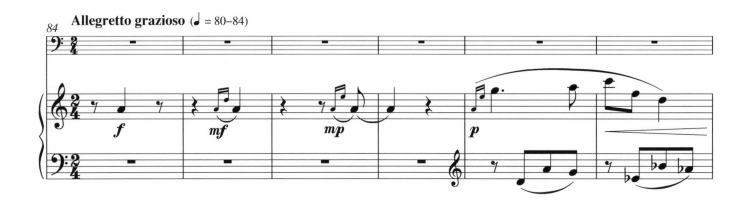

8

Swashbuckler's Song - Lied des Raufbolds

Als Erstausgabe der Sonate erschien eine Kopie von Hindemiths Manuskript.
The first edition of the Sonata was a copy of Hindemith's manuscript.

Paul Hindemith
1895 – 1963

Sonata

für Posaune und Klavier
for Trombone and Piano

Nach dem Text der Ausgabe Paul Hindemith. Sämtliche Werke herausgegeben von /
Edited from the text Edition Paul Hindemith. Sämtliche Werke by
Luitgard Schader

ED 3673
ISMN 979-0-001-04395-3

Posaune / Trombone

www.schott-music.com

Mainz · London · Berlin · Madrid · New York · Paris · Prague · Tokyo · Toronto
© 1942/2015 SCHOTT MUSIC GmbH & Co. KG, Mainz · Printed in Germany

Swashbuckler's Song - Lied des Raufbolds

Allegro pesante ($\senza. = 100–112$)

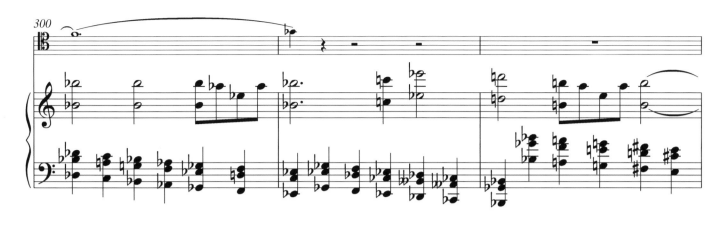

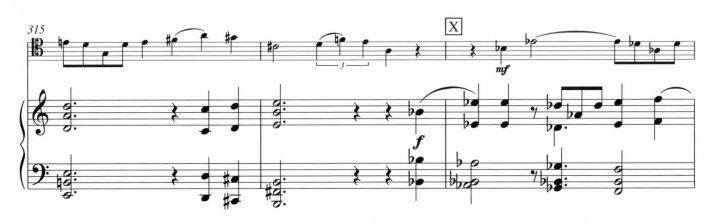

28